And I remember many things ...

Folklore of the Caribbean

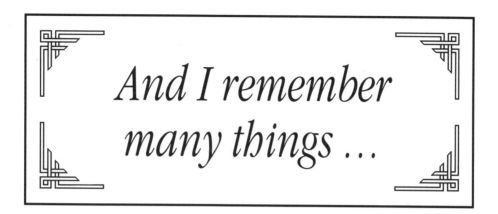

And I remember many things ...

Folklore of the Caribbean

Compiled and Edited by
Christine Barrow

Illustrated by
Wendy Donawa

Collected by
Gracelyn Cassall • Theodore Daniel
Vanessa Greaves • Dorothy Martin

Ian Randle Publishers
Kingston, Jamaica

First published 1992 by
Ian Randle Publishers Limited
206 Old Hope Road, Kingston 6, Jamaica

© 1992 Christine Barrow

Catalogue in Publication data can be found
in the National Library of Jamaica

ISBN 976-8100-14-1

Designed by Susie Home
Typeset by Design & Print, Bromley, UK
Printed by Hollen Street Press, Slough, UK

Contents

FOR

Jennifer and Geoffrey

Josephine and Christopher

Hazel and Carol

Jamie, Andrew and Robbie

Acknowledgement

The Author and Publishers wish to acknowledge with thanks
the assistance of UNICEF, Barbados
whose funding helped to make publication of the book possible.

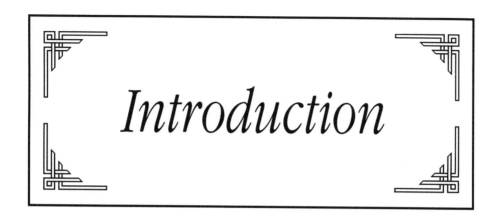
Introduction

Caribbean children today are growing up in a world of television, "fast food" and "ready-mades" – a world dramatically different from that of their grandparents. The purpose of this collection is to preserve some of their heritage for them and for the generations yet unborn.

Christine Barrow • *March 1992*

Story-telling

Sometimes, years ago, neighbours, friends and their children would come here to listen. They would come and I would tell them Anancy Stories. But these days the children don't have the time. They don't look back any more at the old people's sayings. But old people could say some sweet, sweet things. Let me tell you!

Escape from slavery

My grandfather was an African – my father's father. In slavery time the people in the West Indies went up to Africa to buy slaves. My grandfather was one that they bought from Africa and brought down to Guadeloupe.

He wasn't a field worker. The master took him for a groom – to groom the horses. Well, the madam didn't like him. And every day when Massa came home, she "make complain on the man". So the master sent him out into the field to work. Poor man, he didn't understand the field work out there. They used to bang – to beat – the slaves like cattle.

Down here in Antigua the slaves got their freedom before those in Guadeloupe. When they heard that, my grandfather and about six or seven other slaves stole a boat. They sailed it and landed in Antigua, towards Cedar Grove. And my grandfather left there and went to Yorks. He met my grandmother and married her.

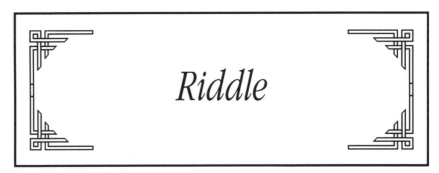

Riddle

Hear what the rich man says:

"If life was a thing
That money could buy,
The rich would live
And the poor would die."

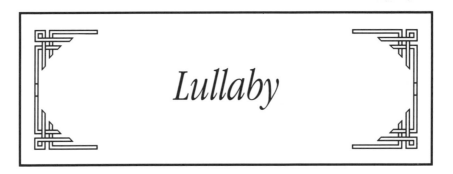

Lullaby

Rock-a-bye baby, on the tree top
When the wind blows, the cradle will rock
When the bough breaks, the cradle will fall
And down will come baby, cradle and all.

Rocking my baby, I know you are sad.
Baby you were naughty, Baby you were bad.
I'm sorry to whip you,
My darling, but true
I'm bound to whip you, for my mama whipped me.

Nicknames

icknames used to be attached to people, sometimes according to what they said.

One day, a boy returned to school after lunch. The teacher asked the children in the class how much of their lunch they had eaten. The boy raised his hand and said, "Teacher, me eat five-eighths ah me lunch".

So he is called "Five-eighths" to this day!

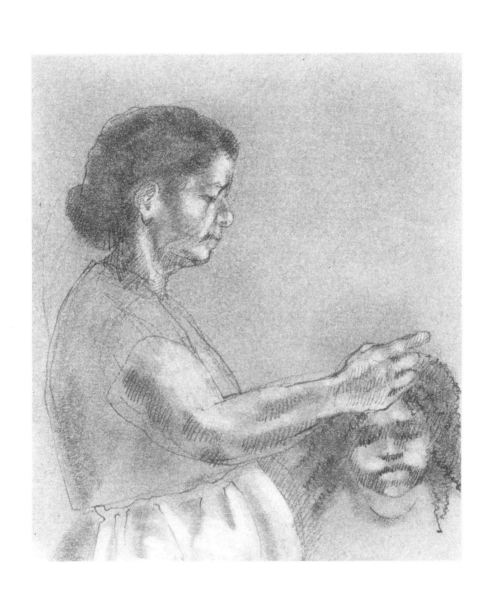

Manners

When my parents were bringing me up, I couldn't meet a big person out there and answer "Yes" or "No" the way I see children doing now. I was telling a little boy that the other morning. He came along with me and was answering "Yes" and "No". So I told him that "Yes" and "No" is really English, but "Yes Sir" and "No Ma'am" is respect. That was respect in my day: that was the style.

You couldn't go to the police station and answer the magistrate with "Yes" and "No". Not you! And we always used the word "Bo" – "Bo John", "Bo this", "Bo that". But not "Massa" – that was for olden slavery time.

Also you couldn't whistle or talk a bad word in front of big people. They would hold you, flog you and then go home and complain to your parents, telling them how you were acting outside. If anybody complained about us, our parents would beat us. But nowadays when children do anything wrong and you complain to their parents, they don't give you any satisfaction.

Food

Our parents would go to the ground where they had their vegetables, to get potatoes. And they would pick coconuts. Then they would send the children to the bay to look for grape leaves.

They grated the potato and the coconut and added sugar and flour. The grape leaves were washed. Then the mixture was put on the grape leaves which were folded like tarts. Using the "bone" or the mid-rib from the coconut leaf, they would pin the grape leaves containing the mixture all around and drop them into boiling water. The leaves would be cooked when they turned colour. They were served with salt fish and spinach.

seagrape

Dressing for tea

We're going now to tea
And you must behave.
For if you don't behave,
You never more shall go.
You spoiled your nice print dress
You tumbled down the stairs
and, oh just tell me dear
What have you now to wear?

Dearie me, dearie me,
Troubles never cease
When we have such bad children,
How can we know much peace?

9

Hard work

My mother was poor and she had no help with us. We had to work very hard. While she was at work, we had to go to the pasture and pick pig food or look for the cattle. And when the weather was dry, we had to carry water for the cattle to drink – up the hill, morning and afternoon. When we got back, we had to sweep the yard, every afternoon. It's true, whatever she sent us to do, we had to do it. She was a very strict mother. We couldn't just go anywhere. We had to obey her. She told us many stories about how her mother had trained her.

I listened to what she had to say and I walked in her footsteps. And now I do the same for my two children, just as she did for me. The most important thing I teach them is the fear of God. Today, parents are filling their children's heads with education. Children want more education, that is good. But education without salvation is nothing at all. I admonish every mother and every father to sit down and teach their children about God. As we look around today, we see what is taking place in this world. Without God we are nothing at all.

Sore foot

In St George's Street, west of the store, was a tavern. It was called "Flying Horse Rumshop".

A boy who used to work there noticed that, at a certain time, the owner would leave the tavern and go home for the night. And at about midnight, a big dog would appear and just walk around.

The boy planned and one night he took a stone and hit the dog one "lick" on his foot. The next morning the owner had one sore foot. The dog was the man!

He used to pretend to be the dog to see if the workers were stealing anything.

Jumbie table

We would always prepare a jumbie table at Christmas time. We had to put a cloth on the table, a white table cloth. And then we cooked a little corn meal, a little rice, dasheen, yam, potato. You could put anything on the table. We boiled salt fish. We put cassava bread and cake. If we killed a pig, we would put a piece of pudding on the table – black pudding.

And we made a plate with some of everything and put a knife and fork and a mug, also a glass full of water. That was for the jumbie. And someone would come and bless the table.

All of this stayed there until Christmas morning. Our grandparents used to tell us that if we took anything off the table, "Jumbie goin' do us something". So we never troubled it, not at all!

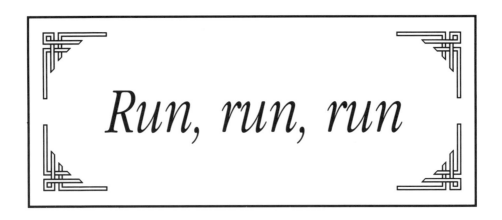

Run, run, run

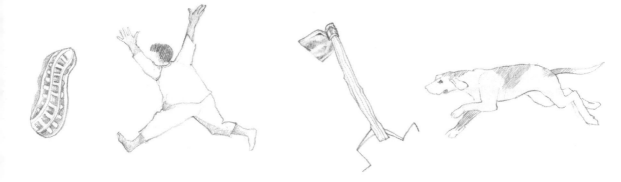

A man planted some nuts in his ground. He said, "I will not reap these nuts until hard-time." But one day, he took up his hoe and said that he would search for his nuts.

And his dog said, "How you say you not goin' dig them 'til hard-time?" He lifted up his hoe to knock the dog.

And the hoe said, "No call to knock 'im, for so you did say". The man threw down the hoe and began to run.

He met a woman with a basket of clothes on her head and she said, "Well, what you a-run for boy?"

He said, "I tek up the hoe to dig the nuts and the dog and the hoe say how I will wait 'til hard-time."

The woman said, "No, that you a-run for?" The basket of clothes on her head said, "If it was you, you would a-run too."

Down she put the basket of clothes and she started to run. The two of them were going until they met another man. The man said, "Is that all you a-kill you'self for?"

And the hoe on his shoulder said, "If me was you, I would-a do the same."

Down with the hoe and all of them run!

Devil's Bridge

T his is the name given to the sea at the eastern end of Antigua. If you drop an egg in the water, it will boil. If you throw a stone in it, it will make a lot of noise. If you whistle, it will get rough.

The sea on Good Friday

P eople believe that it is unsafe to go to the beach and bathe on Good Friday. Stories have been told of people who go to the beach on this day and drown. It is also said that the shoreline recedes a few feet on this special day.

Long life

My father would always tell me, "Boy, you born an old witch. When you born, you born with four teeth in you' mouth. Two a' top and two a' bottom." And I was born with one patch of grey hair. And he would say, "No mid-wife cut you' navel string. You born with you' navel string to length and the mid-wife just tie it." It's true, he told me so.

My father had fourteen of us children and he told me, "You goin' outlive all o' them. You goin' marry, have a wife and have more children than them too."

When he told me these things, I thought he was "talking idleness". At that time I was just a boy and I asked him, "Wha' me study about woman?"

But it's true. I have lived to eighty-one years. None of my brothers and sisters have lived to see this day. My father told me so, told me so when I was a little boy.

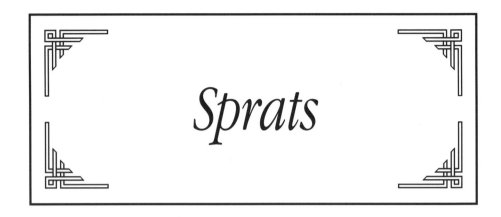

Sprats

In the early days everybody had a fishing boat. Sprats used to be popular, not as a main meal – more as a kind of snack. Sometimes the sprats came in down at the bay and everybody used to go. At that time cooking butter came in five pound tins and people would go down with their butter tins and fill them with sprats according to the size of their families.

At that time we didn't buy fish by the pound. We got a whole parcel of fish for sixpence, four pence, even two pence. We got a big bonito for six pence, what you are paying five and six dollars for now. And if the neighbours didn't have money to buy, then we would cut it up, pass half to them and keep half.

We children, we got tired of cleaning sprats! After we had cleaned them we would "catch up" a fire between three stones. At that time kerosene oil used to come in tall tins and they would give away the tins. We cut them out into four sides, put one piece over the three stones and roasted the sprats on it.

roasting sprats

The sprats used to be seasonal. There was a time for sprats, a time for jacks, a season for bonitos, a season for poy fish. But today fish is not seasonal like it was once. All of a sudden the world has turned over and everything seems to have changed.

Mermaid Rock

resh water runs from Buckley to Big Creek and ends in the sea at Yepton. It was rocky down there and known as Mermaid Rock.

A mermaid is half fish and half mortal and moves under the sea. If a mermaid likes you she will ask you a question. She will ask you if you like "fresh" or if you like "salt".

Now, fish live in the sea and cannot eat anything unless it is salted. And although mermaids live in the sea, they are still fresh. When the mermaid carries you and asks you the question, you have to know what you are supposed to tell her. If you say that you like "fresh", she will eat you because she is fresh. But if you say "salt", she will treat you well. She will cook for you and you will get salt. If you say "fresh" she will kill you, but if you say "salt" she will let you come back home.

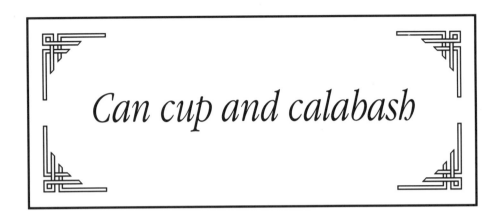

Can cup and calabash

Before gas came in, people had coal pots and clay pots. We put our clay pot on four large stones and built a fire of wood and coconut shells. We scraped out the jelly from the coconut and cut it in two to make calabashes to eat from. Each child had a calabash. And we would take a can to the tinker and let him put on a handle to make a cup. Father and mother had cups and bowls. All of my mother's children had calabashes until they got bigger. Then we got bowls to eat out of.

clay pot

can cup

calabash

Parch corn and molasses

We used to have syrup which our parents got from Mt.Pelier at New Field. Mt.Pelier would grind cane and make molasses.

When we got home from school our parents didn't have anything to give us to eat. And so they would buy this molasses for us. They also had "parch corn" and would mix it with the molasses. Then you would see everybody with their spoons eating "parch corn" and molasses.

We had it hard. But what, it was still better than now.

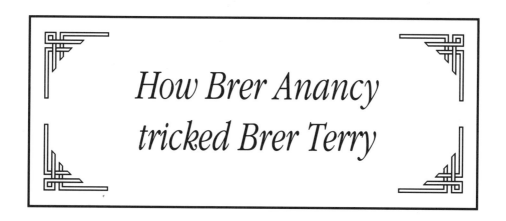

How Brer Anancy
tricked Brer Terry

ne day, Brer Terry visited his brother, Brer Anancy, and he said, "Man, ah run out o' relish and Massa have a lot o' sheep and ley we go tek one, man. Ley we go tek one."

Brer Anancy replied, "Brother, ah rather do things meself. Ah not doing nothing wid you."

But Brer Terry begged him, "Oh Brother, Brother have sympathy. Don't go on so, don't go on so. Man, don't go on so, man. Ley we kill de sheep, ley we go get one o' Massa sheep."

And so they went. They got Massa's sheep and they killed it. Massa now was a slave master, you know. A report reached him that one of his sheep had gone. He suspected that Brer Terry and Brer Anancy were the thieves, but you know, suspicion is not the law. Anyway, Massa was sure that it was the two of them. So he brought a case against them. So they had to go to court. Brer Terry was frightened and he didn't know what to do. He said, "Man, I don't love fo' go a' court at all, at all, at all. When ah go, ah don't know wha' fo' say."

Brer Anancy told him, "Man, after we a' summons we have fo' go, we have fo' appear a' court. We can't go over de law. We have fo' go. Man, you will find something fo' say, man."

Well, you know Brer Anancy had a plan. He said, "We have to try to get away. Man, you nah go a' no jail. Let me tell you now, when de day come fo' we go a' court house, you know wha' I goin' do. Ah go carry me fiddle. Leh me tell you, ah want you to mek a jacket out o' de sheep skin and wear it. And when we get near to de court house, ah goin' play a tune on me fiddle. And when Massa see de skin on you' back, he go see dat a' we got sheep already, so we no have fo' t'ief Massa sheep. An we must get away because of dis skin on you' back."

Brer Terry agreed. He said, "Alright brother, dat's a very good plan, a very good plan, man. Me have on de skin to show how we already got sheep so we could wear sheep skin."

And so the day arrived for them to go to court. As they walked along, a lot of people were there, watching out for them. And Brer Anancy said to Brer Terry, "You know what you do. You have to walk in front o' me and me behind you. And when you hear me get near to de court house, ah goin' play a tune."

But Brer Anancy was planning to trick his brother. The tune that he planned to play was to get Brer Terry into trouble. Brer Anancy wanted people to see that his brother was the thief. Brer Terry had no sense, he was just foolish. Brer Anancy always had more wit than his brother. So they went up to the court house. The people were watching, watching to see what would happen. And Brer Anancy began to play his fiddle, and he began to sing:

> "Oh, me tell Brer Terry,
> "Oh, me tell Brer Terry,
> No fo' t'ief Massa sheep.
> But he wouldn't go by me.
> And the skin on he back
> Will pro-o-o-ove it!"

Small world

When I was small and I looked at the sun and the moon, I really thought that our little island, Nevis, was the world because I couldn't see any other place. But as I grew up, I found out that the world is a big, big place.

Omen

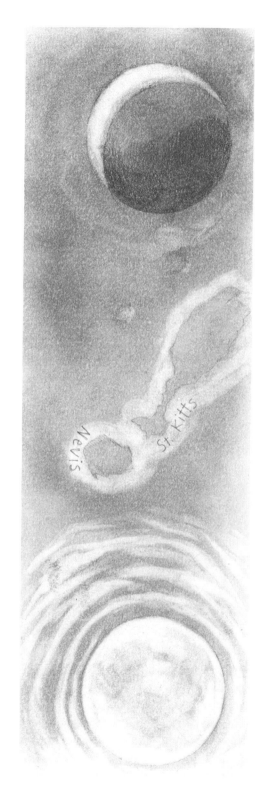

Whensoever you see a fowl come in front of you and start to shake itself out, you are going to get a gift. That is really true. I proved it because it happened to me. The postman came and gave me an order to get a parcel in town.

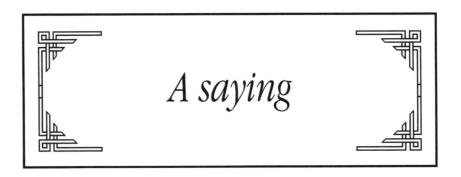

A saying

"**S**tand softly, better than beg pardon." That's what the old people would say. I wondered what it meant and they would explain. If you were a good child, if you do no bad, "no complain come to you". If you don't trouble other children or if your parents sent you out for something and you went and returned quickly, then you "stand softly". But when you were bad, you had to apologise and you would get lashes.

As my mother used to say, "You have fo' go beg pardon. Or de more de lashes dem get under you."

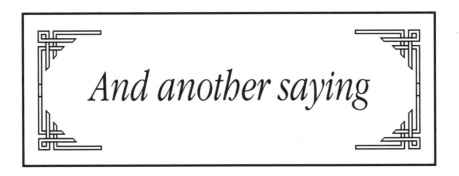

And another saying

The old people would say "Hand come, hand go, roast yam grow." And I would ask my mother how yam could grow if it's roasted. And she would laugh and tell me that it was just a saying. It meant that any kindness you did to others would come back you. People would be kind to you in return.

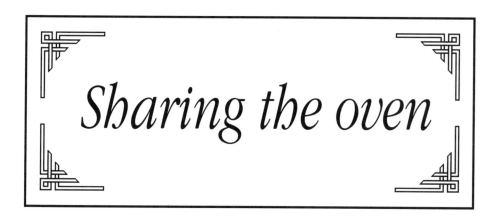

Sharing the oven

I n the early days we had no electricity. There was only one oven and everybody shared it. The neighbours would ask the owner, "Please allow me to bake a cake?" And she would tell you to get ready for such and such a time. You would fix your cakes up to meet that time.

I used to go and bake my cakes with other people too. Two or three people would be waiting there. When they pulled out their bread, you would put in your cakes.

Give and take

In past days people were more free to give. People today don't give unless they get something in return. But people in my early days, they would give and never look back. Especially when it came to Christmas time, they would send rum, cake, bread, bun, all different kinds of things to each other. Those who were wealthier would send a lot of gifts to you at Christmas. They would even send money. Nobody does that today. But I still send to neighbours.

School song

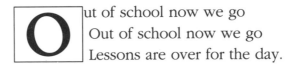

Out of school now we go
Out of school now we go
Lessons are over for the day.

To our homes now we run
To our homes now we run
To work and then to have some fun.

To make a lamp

To make a lamp, you need a bottle and a piece of flour bag. Cut off a thin piece of the flour bag and make a wick. Pour oil in the bottle, push in the wick and light it. And that is your lamp! Things were really bad and poor people had lamps in the early days. But my grandfather was not so poor. He had a lantern.

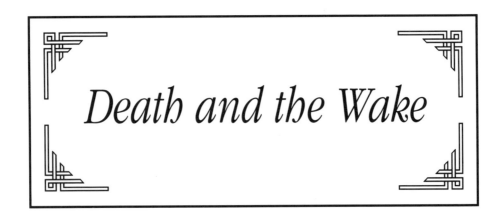

Death and the Wake

I n my young days we never had a morgue, like they have at the hospital now. The dead used to stay at home and we had to bury them very quickly. A member of the family would prepare a plate with a root of grass and rest it on the stomach of the dead. They said that would keep it fresh until the next day. If you dead today, we bury you tomorrow.

And we would keep a wake that night. The neighbours and all the friends of the dead would come to stay with the family. They would prepare coffee or boil up some strong tea with cinnamon bush to keep people awake. Otherwise they would fall asleep. And they would treat them with some biscuits and bread. A special man who understood burial hymns would come and everybody would sing all night.

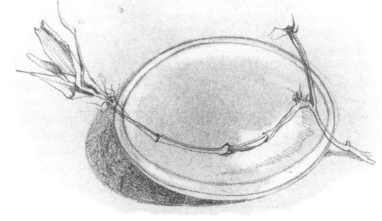

We used to believe

People used to say that, if a funeral
~~eople used to say that, if a funeral~~
was passing and you bent down and
looked between your legs at the coffin,
you would see the dead person sitting
on the coffin. We children used to
believe that and we were afraid. We
would never attempt to do that!

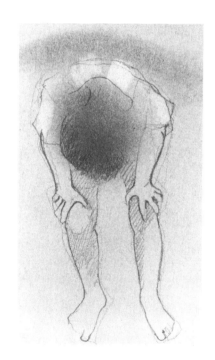

As boys, we used to say,
"You can't point you'
finger in the burial
ground, because you,
finger goin' drop off."

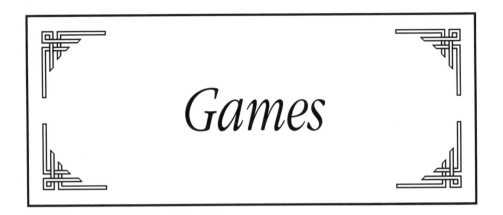

Games

As children we used to play all kinds of games in our neighbourhood in the evenings. When there was moonlight, the girls and boys would hold hands and play ring games and sing all sorts of songs. Or we would have a rope. One child held one end and another the other end and they would turn the rope while someone else jumped in. And we would play rounders or another game called Hoop, which was about hiding and catching and calling "Hoop!"

Action song

The children stand in a long line holding hands, one at the head and the others numbered two, three, four and so on to the tail. To start, the head, without breaking the line, weaves through the arches made by the linked hands of the second and third child, the third and fourth child and so on to the end of the line, to the tail. The children untwist themselves as the game goes along. Then the head moves down the line by changing places with the second child and the process repeats itself until the tail has become the head. The movement is then reversed with the tail leading off, until the head and tail have resumed their original positions. While doing this the children sing:

"Na, Na thread the needle
Nancy, Nancy thread up the needle."

Boy troubles

T ake me back to my mama
Take me as quick as you can
For girl has never known trouble
Until she ties herself to a man.
My boy is like a blue bird
He flies from tree to tree
But now that he's met another girl
He thinks no more of me.

Loose me, Johnny loose me
Loose me, Johnny loose me
Let me go where my mother sends me.

Gal, I wouldn't loose you
Gal, I wouldn't loose you
Can't let you go where your mother sends you.

M y mother has gone to town and she leaves me one at home
She leaves the dogs to bark, to bark to keep those boys
away

    "Hello me dou-dou, hello!"
    You can hello all the time

For my mother has gone to town and she leaves me one at home
She leaves the dogs to bark, to bark to keep those boys away.

Bush Doctors

W e used to have bush doctors.
They knew a lot of things.
They were natural.
They knew the leaves and the combination
of leaves that would bring relief for certain problems.
They would tell you what to mix and what to boil.
And I knew from my experience that it would work.

The bush doctors would say that if you have a
fever inside, lemon grass would help. Worm grass was
for worms and when children were teething, they would
give them worryvine bush. It would bring out their teeth.

Bush medicine was for very poor people. Not for
middle class people, they went to the doctor. The poor
people didn't have money to pay the doctor even though it
wasn't costly at that time – only a shilling or a few pence.

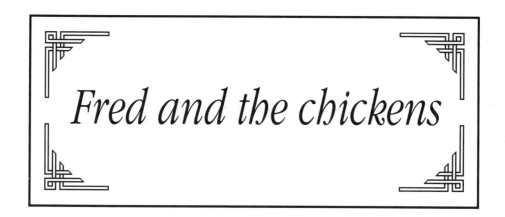

Fred and the chickens

Fred came home from school
As wise as wise could be
And wished to show to all around
How smart a boy was he.

And so at dinner time be began:
"Papa, you think you see
Two roasted chickens on the dish?
Now I will prove it three.
First this is one and that is two
As plain as plain can be
And I was always taught at school
That one and two made three."

And his papa answered just so:
"If what you say is true,
I take one,
Mama takes one
And the third we leave for you."

The boy was so wise that he didn't get any!

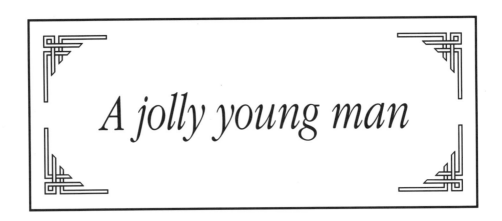

A jolly young man

There was a little man
And he had a little gun
And the bullet was made of lead.
He went to the pond
To shoot some duck
And he shot one in the head
And it dead, dead, dead

He brought it home to the dear old wife
To catch some fire and roast it.
He put it in the kitchen
And it bawled like a chicken
And duck flew away with a quack, quack

Oh boy I am a jolly
Oh boy I am a jolly
Oh boy I am a jolly
I'm a jolly young man.

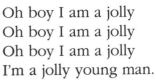

Jack O'Lantern

There was a thing called a Jack O'Lantern. It moved with a light and it shined its light here and there. And it might not shine it again for some time, until it reached all the way down to the west of the village. And then you wouldn't see it again until it reached somewhere else. If it saw anyone while its light shone, it would just go all around, all around. It would shine the light right in your face and then disappear. You wouldn't know where it had gone. The thing is that it would lead you astray. If you were supposed to be going to church, it took you the wrong way. You would just keep walking. And when you "catch yourself", you would be in some thick bush or in a pond. It carried away anybody, any big people who were responsible for themselves. In those days children didn't walk at night so it would never carry them. It started walking at about seven o'clock and continued 'til morning.

43

And you would walk and walk, just following that light. Then it would take off the light and you couldn't see. Some people were witty enough to turn their clothes on to the wrong side or over their heads. They said that would stop it from leading you away.

Jack O'Lanterns don't exist now, but I used to see them.

The first aeroplane

One day when we were coming home from school, we heard this music. When we looked back to see if boys were behind us playing their guitars or drums, we didn't see anybody. And we heard it getting louder and louder. And we started to say to each other, "Judgement coming, judgement coming." And we went home to our parents and told them of the noise we heard in the air.

During the week we heard more music in the air, but we didn't see anything. But then we saw what it was and we ran to hide. It was an aeroplane.

That happened when the first plane came to Antigua.

And the first car

When we were growing up, we were afraid of cars. The first time we saw a car we thought it was a Jack O'Lantern.

People with money had cars. We couldn't own a car. We couldn't even pass and touch their cars.

Houses

We used to live in a "rora house". We would gather the tops of the cane into a pile and dry them. And we would measure out the size of the house with sticks and push the cane tops right down between – pack them tight so that no rain could come in. Then we draped newspapers and so around, inside the house.

A rora house

Some people lived in houses made of wattle and daub. The wattle for the frame of the house came from the forest and the daub was mud. The men who built these houses were paid a shilling a day. They used to call them "stan' off and fire", because they had to stand off and throw the mud on to the frame.

A new house had to be blessed by a preacher. He would say a prayer and a service would be held. Some people would sprinkle water in the four corners of the house. They said this was to get rid of jumbies.

The houses had no floors, "nothing name" concrete or stone cutting. The floor was dirt and the beds were made of sticks and grass. There was no bathroom. We had to go under a tree to bathe. Sometimes we would cut some coconut branches, plait them together and put them around a stick to make it more private.

And there was no kitchen, but sometimes we would make a little shed over some stones, like a pen. And we made a fireplace with three stones to hold the pot for cooking. We washed the dishes with bush – with barsom bush. We had no soap, we just rubbed them hard with ashes.

In those days people didn't have any money. They were poor like church mice.

Walking and hearing

When people had a child who had difficulty walking, they would use bush to rub its knees. Others said that you should go down to the bay and dig a hole in the sand. Let the child stand in the hole and push the sand around its feet. They said that would keep the child's feet close and it would help.

There is also a saying that if a child has poor eyesight, ear-rings would help. Ear-rings were placed in the child's ears and the belief in this superstition sometimes cured the problem.

All these things I heard them say. Up to today some people still believe them.

Jumbies

Once there was a fellow called Willie Taylor who lived in Westbury. He was in love with a woman who lived in Cox Village on the other side of the island. Now, you know in those days fellows used to walk to see their girls, walk for miles.

They would say that if you are walking with someone who can see jumbies and he sees one and "mashes" your heel, you will see it too.

Anyway, this fellow, Willie Taylor, was coming from Cox Village, from his girlfriend. He was travelling home to Westbury, several miles away. He came to a place called Five Turnings – a place between Cotton Ground and Jessops where five roads meet. They used to say that jumbies lived at Five Turnings, so as children we were afraid to pass there.

Well, Willie Taylor reached Five Turnings, late at night. And lo and behold, he saw a jumbie. The jumbie put one foot on each side of the road and Willie could not get across. The jumbie refused to let him pass. This was a fierce jumbie.

Now you know they say that if a jumbie is following you and you are frightened, you should turn your garments on the wrong side – hat on the wrong side, shirt on the wrong side – and the jumbie would be afraid of that.

So Willie took off his hat and put it on the wrong side. Then he took off his shirt and put it on the wrong side to see if the jumbie would be afraid. But this jumbie was a serious fellow and still would not allow him to pass.

Willie decided to trick the jumbie. He said, "Lord, have mercy! Ah wonder when ah goin' reach Bath Village tonight."

Now Bath Village is in the other direction, away from Westbury. So as soon as the jumbie left for Bath, Willie took off full speed for Westbury. He reached home, went in and locked the door behind him quickly. A short time after, the jumbie came up the road, galloping like a horse, rattling his chain. He passed Willie's house, went up the road and came back down, up and down looking for him. But the jumbie couldn't find him and so he got away.

You want to know if this story is true? Well, they used to tell us these stories and as children we would believe them, you know.

"And laugh dem belly full"

While you were out playing in the evening with the other children, sometimes until sleeping time, neighbours would ask you to do any little thing for them. They would say, "Come, come son and do a message here fo' me."

And sometimes they would give you a penny. Sometimes they could only manage a half-penny, but that half-penny would still count a lot because you could go and buy sugarcake or sweeties, something of the sort.

But if they didn't have any money to give you that night, they would tell you that they were going to give you a joke or a 'nancy story. And then we would be so glad. All the children would sit down, fold their arms and "laugh dem belly full".